A SEASON TO BELIEVE

Sports Illustrated

PRESENTS

NEW YORK GIANTS

WORLD CHAMPIONS
SUPER BOWL XLII

Super Bowl MVP
ELI MANNING

THE ALL-NEW ►08■ *CTS*

2008 MOTOR TREND CAR OF THE YEAR™

In today's luxury game, the question isn't about whether your car has a world-class interior. It isn't about available features like all-wheel drive, a 304 hp Direct Injection V6, and a 40-gig hard-drive. It isn't even about industry accolades. No, in today's luxury game, the real question is, when you turn your car on, does it return the favor? Starting at $33,490.* Nicely equipped at $43,380.*

CADILLAC.COM

ELI MANNING, MVP, Champion Quarterback

Skyhawk A-T
Flight Chronograph
Titanium

UNSTOPPABLE.

ELI MANNING IS.
So is his Citizen Eco-Drive.

Fueled by light,
it never needs a battery.

IT'S UNSTOPPABLE.
Just like the people who wear it.

CITIZEN
ECO-DRIVE

citizenwatch.com

©2008 Citizen Watch Company of America, Inc.

THE LINEUP

It was love at first sight for David Tyree and the Super Bowl trophy.

COVER PHOTOGRAPH BY AL TIELEMANS   LINEUP PHOTOGRAPH BY MATTHEW EMMONS/US PRESSWIRE

Sports Illustrated

PRESENTS

SPORTS ILLUSTRATED GROUP Editor Terry McDonell **President/Publisher** Mark Ford **Vice President, Consumer Marketing** John Reese
SPORTS ILLUSTRATED PRESENTS
Editor Neil Cohen **Art Director** Craig Gartner **Senior Editor** Richard O'Brien **Photo Editor** Jeffrey Weig **Editorial Manager** Pamela Ann Roberts
Associate Editors Trisha Blackmar (PROJECT EDITOR), David Sabino **Senior Writers** Damon Hack, Lee Jenkins, Peter King, Tim Layden, Jim Trotter
Writer-Reporter Gene Menez **Reporters** Greg Canuel, Fidencio Enriquez, Joe Lemire, Elizabeth McGarr **Associate Art Director** Karen Meneghin
Associate Photo Editor Kari Stein (PROJECT EDITOR) **Copy Editors** Rich Donnelly, Robert G. Dunn, Jill Jaroff, Denis Johnston, Kevin Kerr,
Anthony Scheitinger, John M. Shostrom **Special Contributor** Pete McEntegart
Vice President, Advertising Sales Richard A. Raskopf **New York Advertising Sales Manager** Garth Rogers **Marketing Associate** Leeann Teager
Time/Warner Retail Arya Abedin, Jim Braia, Liz Burrows, Carrie Frazier, Joseph Kim, Michael Malloy, John McCarthy, Sam Moore,
Eric Szegda, Miguel Yanes

LEADING OFF

A Defense with Teeth

After leading a pep talk before Super Bowl XLII, defensive end Michael Strahan chomped down on the New England offense. The 15-year vet had a sack and helped the Giants limit the Patriots to 274 yards and a season-low 14 points.

III Photograph by JOHN DAVID MERCER/US PRESSWIRE

LEADING OFF

Desert Swarm

With the help of linebacker Kawika Mitchell (55), who had one sack, and defensive end Justin Tuck (91), who had two, New York's relentless defense got its hits on Patriots quarterback Tom Brady, who was sacked five times and hit nine more.

||| Photograph by ROBERT BECK

LEADING OFF

TOUCHING MOMENT

Receiver Amani Toomer, one of two
Giants (along with Michael Strahan)
remaining from the losing Super
Bowl XXXV team, shares the joy after
his six catches helped New York
shock New England 17–14 for the
franchise's third Super Bowl title.

III Photograph by MICHAEL HEIMAN/GETTY IMAGES

A TRI

RECASTING AN IRON GIANT TO

THE NEW YORK GIANTS WALKED AROUND UNIVERSITY OF PHOENIX STADIUM WITH SWEAT ON THEIR BROWS AND JOY IN THEIR EYES. ON THE FINAL SUNDAY OF THE SEASON, THEY DID WHAT NO OTHER TEAM HAD BEEN ABLE TO DO, KNOCKING OFF THE NEW ENGLAND PATRIOTS IN SUPER BOWL XLII IN GLENDALE, ARIZ., AND THE MOMENT PROVED TO BE EVERY BIT AS GOOD

as they had imagined. The game was supposed to be a coronation for the Patriots, who were seeking to join the 1972 Miami Dolphins as the only NFL teams to go undefeated and win the Lombardi Trophy. But New England's march to history was halted by a determined group of Giants who were able to wipe the falling confetti from their faces but not their satisfied smiles after doing the unexpected.

Despite losing to the Patriots by only three in the regular-season finale, New York was a 12-point underdog. The consensus, according to the oddsmakers, was that the Giants had as much chance of beating New England as coach Tom Coughlin did of changing from cold-blooded to warmhearted.

But Coughlin did change. Many of his players point to their coach's transformation as having as big a role in New York's championship run as any pass thrown by Eli Manning

or any sack by Osi Umenyiora.

During his first 11 years as an NFL head coach, Coughlin did it one way: his way. There were no democracies. He was inflexible and intolerant, demanding all that his players had to give but never getting to know them personally or letting them see his true self.

That formula worked well for him in Jacksonville, where he had an expansion team that needed molding and guidance. The Jaguars advanced to the AFC title game in 1996 and had a 14–2 record in '99. But in his first three seasons with the Giants, a team with established veterans who didn't mind questioning the coach's ways, New York had only one winning season and no playoff victories. It was not uncommon for Coughlin to be second-guessed or criticized by some of his players.

The chorus of naysayers intensified after the 2006 season, during which the Giants started 6–2 but finished 8–8,

---

The Lombardi Trophy was a brilliant reflection of Coughlin's new approach. ||| Photograph by TSN/ICON SMI

B U T E

CREATE A CHAMPION *by* JIM TROTTER

then lost in the first round of the playoffs. Some players grumbled privately about Coughlin's unforgiving ways. The exception was star running back Tiki Barber, now retired, who made his complaints public.

Over the years family members, friends and club officials had told Coughlin to lighten up. But it wasn't until last off-season, when the person staring back at him in the mirror said it was time to try something new, that he finally relented.

The 61-year-old coach got the players' attention when he ended off-season workouts by holding a casino night at Giants Stadium for the players and staff. Then during training camp he backed off his grueling practices and even canceled one meeting to take the players bowling. Later, he created his first leadership council, made up of players who have his ear on everything from when and how they practice to what's served at the training table.

"A house divided cannot stand, and that's exactly what my approach was with the team this season," Coughlin said.

"You expect somebody to change a little bit here and there," said defensive end Michael Strahan, a member of the council. "But the changes that he's made have exceeded anything I ever expected to see as long as I've played for him. The guy actually is a personality now. He's funny. He has jokes. He gets the room laughing.

> "THE GUY IS A PERSONALITY NOW," SAYS STRAHAN. "HE MAKES YOU FEEL LIKE YOU CAN ENJOY BEING AT WORK."

He makes you feel like you can enjoy being at work."

As the '07 season progressed, some of the same players who had questioned Coughlin's coaching methods began praising his leadership. They contend that his steadiness and open-mindedness were major factors in the Giants' success.

"When somebody says they're going to change, you always wonder, Well, are they just saying that because it's training camp or it's the off-season?" center Shaun O'Hara said after a midseason win. "But when we were 0–2, he didn't revert back to the way he's always done things. We're talking about a coach who has basically taken everything he's always done and said, 'O.K., I'm going to change.' He almost reinvented himself."

Asked about his transformation in late October, Coughlin chuckled. "What I've done is let them see me as I really am, the good and the bad," he said. "They're also seeing a little more patience on my part. I'm not so quick to fly off the handle, but rather I listen a little bit better.

"From Day One the first thing I did in camp was talk about *team*, to put greater emphasis on the idea that we would only be as successful as we were unselfish and we had to check our egos at the door. That included me. I told the players that I don't really have an agenda. All I want to do is win."

He did just that in Super Bowl XLII, but it wouldn't have happened if he hadn't first won over his players. □

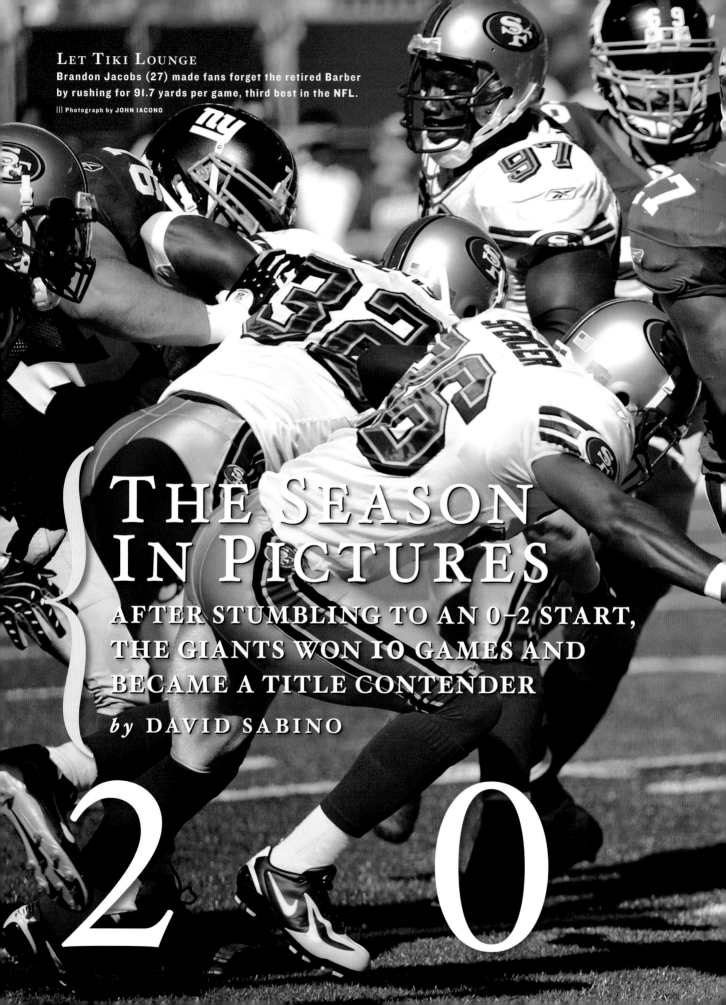

THE SEASON IN PICTURES

AFTER STUMBLING TO AN 0–2 START, THE GIANTS WON 10 GAMES AND BECAME A TITLE CONTENDER

by DAVID SABINO

2 0

07

SEPTEMBER

9

at Irving, Texas

NEW YORK GIANTS   35
DALLAS COWBOYS   45

GAME 1

This fumble recovery by Kevin Dockery (35) set up a field goal that made the score 17–16 at the half, but Tony Romo's four second-half TDs were too much for the Giants to overcome in the highest-scoring meeting of the longtime division rivals.

||| Photograph by
BOB ROSATO

GAME 2 Packers rookie runner DeShawn Wynn was crushed by a Big Blue pile on this carry, but the seventh-round pick scored twice and Brett Favre riddled the Giants' injury-depleted secondary for three more scores en route to his 149th career win.

||| Photograph by CHRIS McGRATH/GETTY IMAGES

SEPTEMBER
23
at Landover, Md.

NEW YORK GIANTS   24
WASHINGTON REDSKINS   17

GAME 3   Sam Madison (six solo tackles, three passes defended) stopped Antwaan Randle-El here, just as the Giants' defense stuffed previously undefeated Washington on a crucial goal-line stand with 20 seconds left to preserve a seven-point win, the team's first of the year.

||| Photograph by GREG FIUME/GETTY IMAGES

SEPTEMBER
30
at East Rutherford
PHILADELPHIA EAGLES 3
NEW YORK GIANTS 16

GAME 4 Plaxico Burress's diving grab, his sixth touchdown in four games, was all the scoring the Giants' offense would need, as Pro Bowl defensive end Osi Umenyiora grounded Eagles quarterback Donovan McNabb for a team-record six of New York's 12 sacks, which tied an NFL mark.

||| Photograph by NICK LAHAM/GETTY IMAGES

OCTOBER
7

at East Rutherford

NEW YORK JETS	24
NEW YORK GIANTS	35

GAME 5

The Jets were tattooing their stadium-mates 17–7 at halftime in the battle for New York supremacy, but Jeremy Shockey and Big Blue pulled away from Gang Green with a 28-point second-half outburst that included Shockey's first score of the year.

||| Photograph by
NICK LAHAM/GETTY IMAGES

at Atlanta
NEW YORK GIANTS 31
ATLANTA FALCONS 10

GAME 6
Rookie cornerback Aaron Ross's value continued to climb as he leaped over two Falcons receivers to snare Joey Harrington's desperation heave at the end of the first half in the Georgia Dome. It was Ross's third interception in two weeks.

||| Photograph by
DOUG BENC/GETTY IMAGES

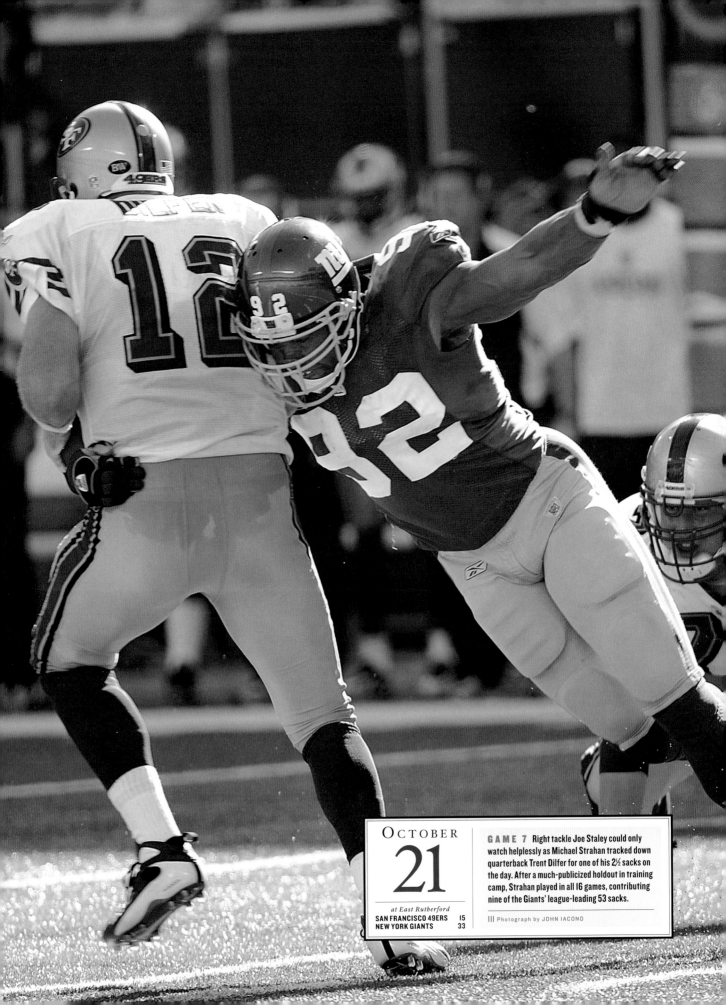

OCTOBER

28

at London, England

NEW YORK GIANTS   13
MIAMI DOLPHINS   10

GAME 8
Despite the pro-Dolphins crowd and the soggy conditions on Wembley Stadium's pitch, left guard Rich Seubert made a surprisingly nimble fumble recovery as the Giants won the first regular-season NFL game played outside North America.

||| Photograph by
BOB MARTIN

NOVEMBER

11

at East Rutherford

DALLAS COWBOYS   31
NEW YORK GIANTS   20

GAME 9

Even with 95 rushing yards from Brandon Jacobs, the Giants fell again to Dallas. Tony Romo threw four more TDs, two to Terrell Owens, for a total of eight for the year—the most ever by a quarterback in one season against New York.

||| Photograph by
JOHN IACONO

NOVEMBER

18

at Detroit

NEW YORK GIANTS 16
DETROIT LIONS 10

GAME 10 James Butler's lone interception of the year was perfectly timed: With 2:04 left and the Lions mounting a comeback, he grabbed this pass intended for Shaun McDonald in the end zone. A pick by Sam Madison 68 seconds later sealed the win.

||| Photograph by JULIAN H. GONZALEZ/ DETROIT FREE PRESS/ZUMA PRESS

NOVEMBER

25

at East Rutherford

MINNESOTA VIKINGS   41
NEW YORK GIANTS   17

GAME 11
The look on his face says it all, as Minnesota's pass rush harassed Eli Manning for three sacks and seven hurries, leading to four interceptions—three of which were returned by the Vikings for touchdowns.

||| Photograph by
RICH KANE/US PRESSWIRE

at Chicago
NEW YORK GIANTS 21
CHICAGO BEARS 16

GAME 12
With New York trailing
16–7 in the fourth to the
reigning NFC champions,
veteran Reuben Droughns,
who was filling in for
injured backs Brandon
Jacobs and Derrick Ward,
helped spur the comeback,
scoring the winning TD on a
two-yard run with 1:33 left.

||| Photograph by
JOHN BIEVER

DECEMBER
9

at Philadelphia
NEW YORK GIANTS 16
PHILADELPHIA EAGLES 13

GAME 13 The Giants rejoiced while Philly kicker David Akers crumbled to the turf in agony after his 57-yard, potentially game-tying field goal with one second remaining caromed off the right upright. The win all but clinched a playoff berth for New York and eliminated the Eagles.

||| Photograph by JEFF ZELEVANSKY/GETTY IMAGES

DECEMBER

16

at East Rutherford

WASHINGTON REDSKINS   22
NEW YORK GIANTS   10

GAME 14
Fred Robbins (98) and the
Giants' D held journeyman
QB Todd Collins to 8-of-25
passing in his first start
since 1997, but Collins still
bested Eli Manning, whose
34 incomplete passes
were a single-game league
high since the AFL-NFL
merger in '70.

||| Photograph by
CHRIS McGRATH/GETTY IMAGES

at Orchard Park, N.Y.

| NEW YORK GIANTS | 38 |
| BUFFALO BILLS | 21 |

GAME 15
Buffalo's Marshawn Lynch was one of the NFL's top rookies in 2007, but he was manhandled on the field by Antonio Pierce (58) and on the stat sheet by Giants seventh-round pick Ahmad Bradshaw, who scored on an 88-yard touchdown run.

||| Photograph by
DOUG BENZ/EPA

DECEMBER
29

at East Rutherford

NEW ENGLAND PATRIOTS 38
NEW YORK GIANTS 35

GAME 16 Eli Manning had his coming-out party in what was predicted to be a meaningless game for the Giants, throwing for 251 yards and four TDs. On the other side of the ball, NFL MVP Tom Brady and Randy Moss set league touchdown records at their positions for the 16–0 Pats.

||| Photograph by DAVID BERGMAN

JANUARY
6

at Tampa

NEW YORK GIANTS 24
TAMPA BAY BUCCANEERS 14

Jeff Garcia came into the game with a 2–0 postseason record against the Giants, but Dave Tollefson & Co. made sure the Bucs' QB ended his day with two interceptions, a 60.5 rating and a loss. End Michael Strahan was also huge on D with nine tackles, a sack and a forced fumble.

||| Photographs by BOB ROSATO

PLAYOFFS

BUCKING THE TREND

by DAMON HACK

WITH ONE MINUTE REMAINing in New York's 24–14 playoff victory over the Tampa Bay Buccaneers on Sunday, Jan. 6, Eli Manning faced one more blind-side rush. As he stood on the sideline, Manning was approached by the Giants' chairman and executive vice president, Steve Tisch, who offered his congratulations to the fourth-year quarterback on his first playoff victory. Coach Tom Coughlin approached Manning as well. Soon the entire Giants sideline was one large receiving line as players and coaches exchanged hugs and high fives on the franchise's first playoff win since January 2001.

"We have good character, and we have good leaders," Coughlin said after the game. "When things go bad, we have some guys who can settle things down. We have some physical toughness, and we have some mental toughness. We have some resiliency."

The Giants needed it all in overcoming a 7–0 deficit following a first quarter in which they gained minus-two yards and appeared headed toward a wild-card playoff loss for the third straight year. Instead, they reeled off 24 straight points to earn the win.

For most of the previous week, the Giants had to confront questions about their shortcomings. Manning had never won a playoff game. Coughlin had never won a playoff game as Giants coach. The Giants entered the game with a –9 turnover margin, while the Buccaneers' was +15. To top it off, New York was facing a Tampa

A more patient Manning earned the first playoff victory of his four-year career.

team with quarterback Jeff Garcia, who was 2–0 against them in the playoffs—a come-from-behind victory five years ago with San Francisco and a grind-it-out win last season with Philadelphia.

But after giving up a touchdown on Tampa's second possession, the Giants' defense started suffocating Garcia into mistakes. He threw two interceptions and made several off-balance throws as the pocket started to collapse around him. Garcia finished the day 23 of 39 for 207 yards and had a 60.5 quarterback rating. (Manning was 20 of 27 for 185 yards, two touchdowns, no interceptions and a 117.1 quarterback rating.)

An underlying theme leading up to the game had been each team's preparation in the final week of the season. Tampa Bay coach Jon Gruden decided to rest many of his starters, while Coughlin sent his best out to try and derail the New England Patriots' perfect season. As it turned out, the Giants might have won this game because of confidence gained from their sturdy showing in the 38–35 loss to New England.

After an 0–2 start, a six-game winning streak and some choppy play in the second half of the season, New York was peaking at the right time, and Manning looked as comfortable as ever in a Giants uniform. He exhibited patience and poise against Tampa's opportunistic defense.

"Everybody stepped up and had a role," Manning said. "All of our running backs, tight ends, receivers, special teams. But now you can't just be satisfied with what you're doing. It's about the bigger picture and keeping this thing going." □

HITTING PAY DIRT
Brandon Jacobs, the Giants' top rusher in the regular season, barreled into the end zone for two second-quarter scores.

TANGLED UP IN BLUE
Linebacker Reggie Torbor kept Tampa Bay's Earnest Graham from getting a leg up. The Giants held the Bucs to 69 yards rushing.

CAUGHT RED-HANDED
Plaxico Burress strong-armed Ronde Barber for one of the wideout's four receptions. In all, seven players made catches for New York.

JANUARY

13

at Irving, Texas

NEW YORK GIANTS 21
DALLAS COWBOYS 17

Dallas safety Roy Williams could only watch as Amani Toomer scooted up the sideline en route to this 52-yard first-quarter touchdown. The 12th-year receiver scored again on a four-yard toss from Eli Manning with seven seconds left in the first half to tie the score at 14.

||| Photograph by
JOHN W. McDONOUGH

LEAVING THE PAST BEHIND

by DAMON HACK

THE HEALING BEGAN AT A BLACKJACK table, of all places, in a banquet room at Giants Stadium in the middle of baseball season. A June minicamp had come to an end, but New York Giants players and coaches were instructed to convene for one last meeting before going their separate ways. Seated at the table, carrying neither a whistle nor his familiar scowl, was coach Tom Coughlin, waiting for face cards. It was a team-only casino night, the first in Coughlin's four-year tenure and an uncharacteristic off-season overture from the coach to his players.

The gamble paid off big. "It gave us a chance to see him as something other than just Coach Coughlin, standing at the podium, giving a speech," defensive back R.W. McQuarters says. "We put football to the side. We were just guys."

Since then the Giants have found common ground with their coach, created magic in a season that began in peril and, on Jan. 13, crushed the Super Bowl hopes of hated rival Dallas on its own field. Against the Cowboys at Texas Stadium, facing tall odds and playing on weary legs, New York scripted a remarkable afternoon that culminated in a 21–17 victory and a berth in the NFC title game at Green Bay.

Even as Dallas mounted one last drive, reaching the Giants' 23-yard line with less than a minute to play, New York linebacker Antonio Pierce pulled his teammates close for final instructions and some late inspiration. "Nobody gave us a chance," Pierce reminded his mates. "Nobody thought we would be here."

McQuarters (center) celebrated his game-saving pick with his Giants mates.

||| Photograph by JOHN W. McDONOUGH

With 16 seconds left and the Cowboys facing fourth-and-11, Tony Romo whistled the ball toward receiver Terry Glenn in the end zone. When McQuarters stepped in front and intercepted the pass, the visitors' sideline erupted, Coughlin and his men celebrating the Giants' first trip to a conference title game since the 2000 season.

Dallas had twice decked the Giants on its way to the NFC East title, but in the third meeting it was New York that delivered the knockout. After Romo lit up the Giants for eight TDs in the regular season, keeping many plays alive with his feet, New York added several blitzes to its pressure package. The Giants sacked Romo twice in the fourth quarter and harassed him to the point that the defensive line could hear him as he tried to make adjustments. "I think he was getting a little worried," said defensive end Osi Umenyiora. "He was telling Marion Barber to chip [block] me."

Afterward, the Giants dressed amid laughter, Pierce asking for popcorn with butter and salt, a reference to Dallas wideout Terrell Owens's oft-mentioned snack recommendation. McQuarters walked off clutching the football he'd snagged from Romo, planning to give it to his son, Rylan Wynter, who turned eight that day. One after another the Giants followed him toward the team buses, their ninth straight road win behind them, underdogs chugging north toward Lambeau.

"I heard we were supposed to be scared," guard Chris Snee said, lobbing one last volley toward the Cowboys. "There was no one scared in this locker room, and there will be no one scared next week." □

POCKET PROTECTION
Brandon Jacobs (27), David Diehl and
Rich Seubert made Manning's poised
play (163 yards, 2 TDs) possible.

||| Photograph by BOB ROSATO

BREAKING THROUGH
Ahmad Bradshaw (44), a seventh-round draft pick, came on strong late in the year.

||| Photograph by PETER READ MILLER

CRUNCH TIME
Romo's Mexican holiday with Jessica Simpson had him feeling the heat, but that was nothing compared to this encounter with Umenyiora.

||| Photograph by PETER READ MILLER

Against Green Bay, Burress, playing with a torn ligament in his right ankle, produced the game of his life—and the greatest playoff game ever for a Giants receiver—a gutty and intimidating performance that included 11 catches for 151 yards.

||| Photograph by JOHN BIEVER

ROAD TO THE SUPER BOWL

N F C   C H A M P I O N S H I P | *Giants   vs.   Packers*

A STONE-COLD CLASSIC

by PETER KING

BRETT FAVRE AND ELI MANNING MET for a private moment at midfield before the NFC Championship Game at the Lambeau Icebox on Jan. 20, and the old lion leaned in to get close to the kid. You could only imagine what they were saying to each other—something about enjoying the moment because you never know when another one will come, perhaps, or how odd it was for two sons of the South to be playing in one of the coldest games in history.

Not exactly.

"Peyton here?" Favre asked.

"Nah," Eli said. "He didn't make it."

The NFL didn't need the elder Manning to stage one of the best playoff games in years. His kid brother did just fine.

The lead changed frigid hands four times before the Packers tied the game at 20 in the fourth quarter. After missing field goal tries from 43 yards (high snap) and 36 (inexcusable knuckleball) in the final 6:53 of regulation, New York kicker Lawrence Tynes won it with a 47-yarder in OT. Eli stepped out of Peyton's shadow with a 21-for-40, 254-yard passing performance that moved the chains. Plaxico Burress had the greatest playoff game ever for a Giants wide receiver, catching 11 passes for 151 yards and embarrassing Pro Bowl cornerback Al Harris—all while playing with a torn ligament in his right ankle.

It was take-your-breath-away drama. Favre pump-faking, play-acting and finally throwing one deep to Donald Driver for a 90-yard touchdown; Giants cornerback R.W. McQuarters picking off Favre but having the

Despite the chill, Michael Strahan and Manning basked in the glow of victory.

||| Photograph by SIMON BRUTY

ball popped from his arms right into the breadbasket of Packers tackle Mark Tauscher; Favre throwing away the game on an easy interception by corner Corey Webster 47 seconds into overtime. New York sent out its bruising running backs—mighty mite Ahmad Bradshaw, the 250th of 255 players selected in the 2007 draft, colliding helmet-to-helmet with a Packers defender so violently that the impact stripped much of the paint off Bradshaw's helmet; and 264-pound freighter Brandon Jacobs, plowing first into cornerback Charles Woodson, who was sent sprawling, and then into middle linebacker Nick Barnett, who was driven back five yards.

It was the kind of football you watch and wince at. "Mano a mano," Burress said. "Two great teams, just trying to survive on the coldest day any of us have played on."

In fact, it was the third-coldest game in NFL history, registering –1° with a –23° windchill at kickoff. One player seemed immune to the conditions. For reasons even he could not fathom, Burress's game was largely unaffected by the cold. Playing with heat pads taped to the bottom of his socks, he caught passes behind, in front of and over Harris, once stealing a jump ball from him. In the third quarter Burress caught a pass and survived a Jack Tatum–force hit from safety Atari Bigby, holding on to the ball. Burress jawed with Harris. He squawked at the Packers' sideline. Time after time he wrestled with Harris past the five-yard bump zone, skirmishes that were often overlooked by the officials. He played the game of his eight-year pro career, gutty and physical and intimidating. □

MIGHTY MITE

The 5′ 9″ rookie Bradshaw played big against the Pack, busting through the Green Bay defense for 63 yards on 16 carries.

||| Photograph by JOHN BIEVER

THROWAWAY MOMENT

Webster's interception of this errant Favre toss, designated for Driver, 47 seconds into overtime set the table for the Giants' victory.

||| Photograph by PETER READ MILLER

THIRD TYNES THE CHARM

After missing earlier field goal tries from 43 yards and 36 yards in the final 6:53 of regulation, Tynes won redemption—and the game—with this 47-yarder in overtime, earning a warm locker-room greeting from coach Tom Coughlin.

||| Photographs by SIMON BRUTY (above) and DAVID J. PHILLIP/AP

* If she hadn't signed up at match.com, they would never have met at the Bronx Zoo for their first date, watched documentaries all night, planned a trip to South Africa, eaten too many local sticky donuts called koeksisters, decided against a tour guide, discovered that the Southern Hemisphere had a completely different set of stars and fallen asleep exhausted in the front of their rental truck.

START YOUR OWN LOVE STORY TODAY AT

match.com®

SUPER BO

{ # PERFECTLY IMPERFECT

THE GIANTS SHOCKED THE 18–0 PATRIOTS BY BEING THE BETTER TEAM IN THE BIGGEST GAME OF THE SEASON

by TIM LAYDEN

W L X X L I I

FEBRUARY

3

at Glendale, Ariz.

NEW YORK GIANTS   17
NEW ENGLAND PATRIOTS   14

Banged around all night by Tuck (91), Strahan (92) and the rest of the Giants' wrecking crew, Brady was sacked five times and hit nine more. Though he had thrown a league-record 50 TDs in the regular season, the NFL's MVP managed just one against New York.

||| Photograph by WALTER IOOSS JR.

THIS TIME THE CELEBRATION WAS FOR THE YOUNGEST CHILD OF A FOOTBALL FAMILY AND FOR THE TEAM HE HELPED CARRY

TO AN UNLIKELY CHAMPIONSHIP. A YEAR AGO IN MIAMI, ELI MANNING HAD SEEN HIS OLDER BROTHER PEYTON TRANSFORMED BY A SUPER BOWL CHAMPIONSHIP. HE HAD SEEN PEYTON WALK INTO HIS OWN VICTORY PARTY SO BLISSFULLY SATISFIED THAT

the moment found a place in Eli's soul and changed him as well. "It put a hunger inside me," Eli says. "You always want to win, but after that I felt like I wanted it even more." And now, so soon afterward, it would be his turn.

A second-floor restaurant at the New York Giants' team hotel outside Phoenix had become a thrumming nightclub into early Monday morning, a steady bass beat providing the backdrop to the unmistakable buzz of victory shared with friends and family at another Manning Super Bowl celebration. One floor below, some Giants players and a horde of the

Brandon Jacobs used his brawn to gain a critical fourth-quarter first down.

||| Photograph by AL TIELEMANS

team's supporters filled a massive ballroom for another party, and outside in the night a long line of cars snaked nearly the full two miles from the Sheraton Wild Horse Pass Resort in Chandler, Ariz., to Interstate 10 as the desert sky spit raindrops and high winds buffeted the sagebrush along the highway. Drivers wore Big Blue jerseys and wanted only a piece of the delirium.

It was to have been a historic night. The New England Patriots would win their 19th consecutive game and become only the second NFL team, along with the 1972 Miami Dolphins, to complete a season unbeaten and untied. They would fortify the legacy of a modern professional dynasty with a fourth Super Bowl title in seven years. They would prove themselves perfect.

Instead, the Giants completed an unexpected and emotional postseason run with a 17–14 victory in Super Bowl XLII. It was history cut from another cloth, a performance built on the sturdy underpinnings of a

ferocious defensive effort, sustained when quarterback Manning and wide receiver David Tyree combined on one of the most memorable plays in NFL history and sealed when Manning threw a 13-yard touchdown pass to Plaxico Burress with 35 seconds to play. The game will take its place not only as the second-greatest upset in a Super Bowl—behind the New York Jets' epic 16–7 defeat of the Baltimore Colts in January 1969—but also as the culmination of a season in which a team, a quarterback and a coach found themselves linked by a deep resilience and rode it to the top of their sport.

Here in the afterglow Manning, the game's MVP, worked the room, bouncing among groups of friends: those from Isidore Newman, his New Orleans high school; from Ole Miss, where he played his college ball; and from New York. His mother, Olivia, stood talking with Eli's fiancée, Abby McGrew. Peyton remained in the back of the room, ceding the stage to Eli. "It's just surreal," Eli said over the noise. Past midnight he joined with his oldest brother, Cooper, and together they sang. The selection, of course, was *New York, New York*.

T HROUGHOUT THE WEEK LEADING UP TO Super Bowl XLII, the Giants were loose, the Patriots smooth yet practiced. For Tom Brady, coach Bill Belichick, wideouts Randy Moss and Wes Welker, linebackers Tedy Bruschi and Junior Seau, this was another day at work. The Super Bowl

---

Manning was in Super form, leading the game-winning drive and earning MVP honors. ||| Photograph by AL TIELEMANS

Amani Toomer lunged to make this 38-yard catch in the second quarter, but the Giants failed to score on the drive.

||| Photograph by DAMIAN STROHMEYER

would be either a coronation or a colossal upset; it would not simply be an NFL title game. The Patriots had spent the entirety of their 16–0 regular season, including a riveting 38–35 win over the Giants on Dec. 29, and their run through the AFC playoffs denying their pursuit of history, but that larger task defined the game. Some of the New England players even admitted it. "You have to finish," Seau said in midweek. "You have to finish, or it doesn't count to be in that 'great' group."

The Giants, who were 10–6 in the regular season and the fifth seed in the NFC playoffs, slowly grew sick of their role. "Everywhere you went, it was all about the Patriots and 19–0," said cornerback R.W. McQuarters after the game. "We go into the city, and there's Tom Brady on the buildings. We get to the stadium today, and there's a Super Bowl program in our locker, and it's like a Tom Brady magazine. We come out to warm up, and Tom Brady is on the big screen. It's like Tom Brady was everywhere."

In the December home loss to New England, New York gave up 22 points in the final 19 minutes; Brady passed for 356 yards, including a 65-yard bomb to Moss for the go-ahead score. But the Giants' defensive front—ends Osi Umenyiora, Justin Tuck and the unit's veteran leader, Michael Strahan, and tackles Barry Cofield and Fred Robbins—had pressured Brady all night, despite sacking him only once. "We did some things really well against them the first time,"

said Tuck. "We just didn't get him on the ground."

They did on Sunday. Mixing A-gap blitzes from weak-side linebacker Kawika Mitchell with steady four-man pressure from the line, the Giants brought relentless heat to the highest-scoring offense in NFL history. New York had five sacks and hit Brady nine other times. Central to the effort was Tuck's constant movement, making it difficult for Brady to identify where the rush was likely to come from. ("The Jets did that to them near the end of the season, and it looked like Brady had a hard time," said Tuck). The Giants manhandled the Patriots' offensive line, which includes three Pro Bowl players, and limited tailback Laurence Maroney, who had 244 rushing yards over two playoff games, to 36 yards on the ground. All-Pro left tackle Matt Light was beaten repeatedly by Umenyiora and spooked into two false starts in the second half.

The upshot of all this defense—New England's unit also played solidly—was a brutal game in which, after the Patriots took a 7–3 lead on the first play of the second quarter, the two teams went 33 minutes, 52 seconds without scoring, a Super Bowl record. Then they played a 15-minute masterpiece, compressing a night's drama into the fourth quarter.

First, Manning threw a touchdown pass to Tyree with 11:05 to play. Three series later Brady completed 8 of 11 on an 80-yard drive, capping it with a six-yard TD pass to Moss that put New England back on top 14–10 with 2:42 remaining. The game rested in Manning's hands.

The picture is only half the story.

Get the full home theater experience with Bose® sound.

The creak of a floorboard behind you. The roar of a crowd around you. It's sound that brings movies, sports and music to life. Bose Lifestyle® home theater systems are engineered with unique technologies to reproduce sound with vivid detail. Because room size, shape and furnishings can make even the most expensive system sound like one worth half the price, Lifestyle® systems customize the sound to fit your room. So you hear rich, accurate surround sound. Plus, they can be expanded to deliver music throughout your home, even outdoors. Hear one of our premium home theater systems for yourself, and you may be surprised by what you've been missing.

NEW Lifestyle® 48 Series IV
DVD home entertainment system

Designed for those who want a complete entertainment system. Includes built-in DVD/CD player, up to 340 hours of music storage and patented uMusic® intelligent playback system.

NEW Lifestyle® V30 home theater system

Designed for those who want to select their own DVD player and other entertainment sources. Makes it easy to connect multiple audio and video components, and then hide them from sight.

1-800-434-2073, ext.5053 Bose.com/lifestyle
Call or visit us online. And discover why Bose is the most respected name in sound.

TO NEW YORK FANS AND MEDIA, MANNING had been the biggest of targets for more than three seasons. Blame for any fresh failure inevitably was laid at his feet, until he directed the wild-card Giants to January playoff wins at Tampa Bay, Dallas and then frigid Green Bay in the NFC Championship Game. Slowly New York began to embrace its quarterback. Two days after the win over the Packers, Manning had dinner with friends at Rao's, a popular Italian restaurant in East Harlem. While he was in the restroom, owner (and *Sopranos* regular) Frank Pellegrino announced to the diners that Eli was in their midst, and when the quarterback emerged he was given a standing ovation. He got another one as he left.

Yet Manning had been neither brilliant nor bad in the first three quarters of the Super Bowl. When he took the field for what would be the defining drive of his career, he was 14 of 25 for 178 yards with one touchdown and one interception. The Giants took six plays to move from their 17-yard line to their 44, where, on third-and-five, Manning took a shotgun snap and carved a place in football lore. Quickly swarmed in a collapsing pocket, he was grabbed by the Patriots' Jarvis Green, a 6' 3", 285-pound defensive end. For an instant Manning disappeared, presumed sacked. Somehow, though, he pulled away from the scrum. His mother watched and was transported back nearly four decades, to a time when her sweetheart was tearing up the Southeastern Conference with a freewheeling quarterbacking style. Said Olivia, "That looked like Archie running around at Ole Miss."

Once free, Manning squared himself and lobbed a pass into the middle of the field toward Tyree, who

Strahan and the Giants' linemen seemed to come at Brady from every angle. ||| Photograph by AL TIELEMANS

Here's to You on a
GIANT
Accomplishment

Congratulations to the World Champion
New York Giants

STOP&SHOP®

Manning's 45-yard toss to rookie Kevin Boss at the start of the fourth quarter set up the Giants' first TD.

||| Photograph by HEINZ KLUETMEIER

had stopped after running a post pattern. A fifth-year wideout best known for his special teams work, Tyree scarcely fit the hero's mold—he had caught only four passes in the regular season and one in the playoffs. But Manning likes Tyree. After a disastrous Friday practice in which Tyree had dropped a half-dozen passes, Manning went up to the receiver and told him, "You forget about this. You're a gamer. I know you are."

With the Super Bowl in the balance, Tyree rose high and outfought Patriots veteran strong safety Rodney Harrison, clutching the ball against his own helmet. "Harrison is a dirty cheap-shot artist and also a heck of a football player," said Tyree. "But once that ball was in the air, it was mine, mine, mine, like a little kid." The 32-yard gain—Harrison called it "a Hail Mary"—took

the ball to the New England 24-yard line. Three plays later Manning threw 12 yards to rookie Steve Smith for a first down at the Patriots' 13 with 39 seconds left.

The Giants' next formation sent Burress to the left. He was all alone, and not for the first time. The eighth-year veteran had isolated himself on the Monday before the game, casually tossing out a prediction to the *New York Post* that the Giants would win the game 23–17. While that collected mountains of attention, Burress quietly struggled physically. After playing most of the season on a sprained right ankle, he slipped in the shower on the Tuesday morning of Super Bowl week—"a freak accident," he called it. When he was told that he had injured the medial collateral ligament in his left knee, "I busted out crying," said Burress. "I

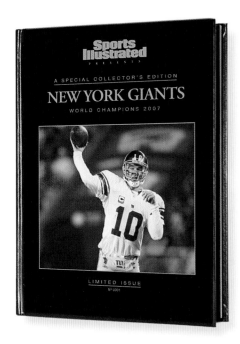

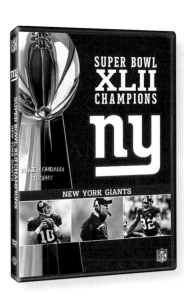

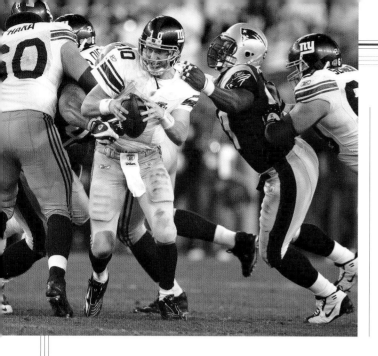

In the game's defining moment Manning channeled his father to escape a sure sack, then threw to Tyree (85), who outdueled Harrison for the 32-yard catch.

||| Photographs by BOB ROSATO (left) and DAMIAN STROHMEYER

thought I wasn't going to be able to play in the biggest game of my life." He didn't practice again before the game and said, "I didn't even run until [Super Bowl Sunday]."

But on the deciding play, the Patriots blitzed, leaving cornerback Ellis Hobbs in single coverage on Burress. Hobbs guessed slant—"He pretty much has to guess one way or the other," said Peyton—the play called for a fade, and Hobbs was badly beaten. "End of story," said Eli.

Or perhaps the beginning. A year ago Manning was at the center of a Giants collapse during which the team dropped six of its final eight in the regular season and lost in the first round of the playoffs. Manning's leadership was criticized by retired New York running back Tiki Barber, in his role as an analyst for NBC, and the quarterback was under intense scrutiny from fans and media. For now, he is set free. "I've had a lot of downs in New York," Eli said, as he stood to the side at his victory party. "A lot of times I've thought, Why have I gotten this treatment? Do I deserve this? So to come out here and win, not just for me but for our whole team, is really special. And for me personally, I'd have to say it is kind of sweet."

B Y THE TIME THE SUPER BOWL kicked off, it was old news that coach Tom Coughlin's personality shift—from dour disciplinarian to back-slapping players' coach—was a significant part of the team's rise. For those closest to Coughlin, the issue is far less complex. "We've always known who our dad is," said Tim Coughlin, 35, a Wall Street bond trader and the second of Tom's four grown children. "And we've all seen what he had to go through."

Like Manning, the 61-year-old Coughlin had been pilloried by fans, media and Barber. Like Manning, he felt the heaviest blows in the wake of the Giants' '06 collapse.

OWN A PIECE OF SPORTS HISTORY

SI Cover Collection - Choose from over 1,500 reprints of current and classic Sports Illustrated® covers

11" x 14" photo quality reprints ■ Available framed and unframed

www.SIcovers.com

Burress (above) hauled in the winning score with 35 seconds left. The Giants' defense held, leaving Manning one last snap before the party could start.

||| Photographs by BOB ROSATO (above) and ROBERT BECK

"My father was hurt by the criticism last year and in the off-season," said Tim, as he stood on the field at University of Phoenix Stadium in the aftermath of the Giants' victory. "And that's what makes this night so special for our family and for him."

In the weeks and months to come, the Giants will be celebrated as only a precious few cities can lift a champion. Coughlin, Manning, Burress, Strahan and the rest will hear many more ovations. To the north the Patriots will answer questions about their two-drive Super Bowl. About the meaning of winning 18 games but finishing with a loss. About history denied.

But beneath a dome in the desert on the evening of Feb. 3, time was the province of the winners. Players lingered with family. In the stands scattered groups of Giants fans chanted mockingly, "Eighteen-and-one . . . eighteen-and-one." On the battered grass two of Coughlin's grandchildren, four-year-olds Emma and Dylan, lay on their backs and swept their arms and legs, making snow angels in the confetti. The only word to describe the scene would be: *Perfect.* □

SI.COM gets you inside the game 24/7.

Congratulations
TO THE
New York Giants

SUPER BOWL
XLII
Champions

from all of your "Super" fans!

FINDING THE GIANT WITHIN

IN A NEW YORK MINUTE ELI MANNING CAME OF AGE THIS SEASON AND LED HIS TEAM TO A SUPER BOWL CHAMPIONSHIP

by DAMON HACK

ELI MANNING WAS TOO YOUNG TO REMEMBER THE SUNDAY NIGHTS when his father, Archie, walked through the front door, carrying the burdens and bruises from an afternoon of losing in the NFL. Archie would gather Eli's older brothers, Cooper and Peyton, on the couch and have them participate in a regular competition: Who could best massage the bumps and knots out of daddy's aching arms and shoulders? ¶ Eli would learn about burdens and bruises soon enough, though. He followed Archie and Cooper to Ole Miss and Peyton to the NFL, the youngest, quietest Manning boy having to live up to impossible expectations. Just when it looked like Manning might never reach the level expected of the top pick in the draft, he surprised fans and detractors alike by engineering a turnaround that will make him a New York legend. On the road in Tampa, in the hostile confines of Texas Stadium, on the frigid ice of Green Bay and, finally, in the Arizona desert against the undefeated New England Patriots, Eli Manning grew up right before the nation's eyes. ¶ With Manning directing the offense, the Giants reeled off 11 consecutive road victories to conclude

Manning let his emotions show during the playoff win over Tampa Bay.

||| Photograph by RICH KANE/US PRESSWIRE

the season, including a 17–14 victory over the Patriots in Super Bowl XLII. With one magical playoff run, he emerged from the considerable shadow of his father and brother, carving a niche as a star in his own, shy way.

Before the 2007 season, following three up-and-down years in the league, Eli took a shot from his former running back Tiki Barber, who questioned his skills as a leader and called his motivational speeches "almost comical." Manning then spent much of the regular season fluttering passes off his back foot, throwing 20 interceptions (tied for the league

in the locker room or your approach. You have to stay the same and have a good attitude about everything and show everybody that it doesn't bother you and doesn't affect you and you are going to go out there and still practice hard and perform hard."

Says head coach Tom Coughlin, "He is very resilient. He is very focused on his job. He never bats an eye about saying what his responsibilities are or whether he performed well or not. He is an elected captain on the team. He is fully aware of that responsibility as well."

Growing up in a hypercompetitive family, Manning

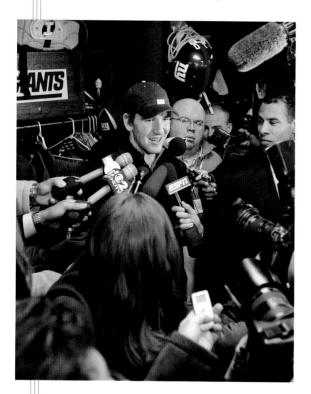

OVER A FOUR-GAME STRETCH MANNING FINALLY STOOD ALONE, HIS EXPECTATIONS MET, HIS STATUS AS A NEW YORK LEGEND SECURE.

Amid pressure from the media, Archie (above) helped Eli keep his spirits high.

high) and earning the wrath of many New York fans.

At various points during the season, angry Giants fans called into sports talk radio stations, asking if their quarterback would ever mature into a winner. Would he ever be accurate enough? Why wasn't he more emotional? Would the Giants ever bench him for backup Jared Lorenzen?

If Manning ever heard the shouting, he says it never got him down. In victory and defeat, he offered a poker face, punching the clock and saying little.

"You just have to learn to accept it," Manning says of the criticism. "It happens after a loss sometimes. You never know when it is going to happen or what is going to cause it or what strikes it up. But it is out there, and you can't let it affect your personality or the way you are

had to be resilient. His father and brothers dominated the dinner table conversation and the backyard football games, while Eli mostly stayed out of the way. When his brothers graduated high school and were out of the house, Eli spent a lot of time with his mother, Olivia, and seemed to adopt her quiet demeanor.

But Peyton said he never doubted that Eli had the makeup to be a Super Bowl champion. "When I call him on Tuesdays, on his off day, he is always at the facility lifting weights or studying film," Peyton says. "When I call him on Wednesday nights or Thursday nights, what is he doing? He is always studying film. As a quarterback, I just can't tell you how much I appreciate that kind of work ethic, because I'm very much in the same mode. I can just tell how seriously he takes his profession. I can tell how disappointed he is when I talk to him after a game on Sunday that they haven't won. He feels accountable."

In the playoffs Manning's preparation produced unmistakable results. Before facing Tampa Bay, Eli called Peyton and asked him for advice on going against such an aggressive defense. The Colts had beaten the Bucs, 33–14, in Week 5. Peyton's instructions to Eli were clear.

"Be patient and take the short stuff," Eli says Peyton told him.

Manning battled frigid temperatures and the Packers' pass defense to lead the Giants to a 23-20 overtime win in the NFC Championship Game.

Eli responded by completing 20 of 27 passes for 185 yards, two TDs and no interceptions in a 24–14 victory.

Against the Dallas Cowboys, who had twice beaten the Giants in the regular season, Manning led one of the best drives of his career. With 47 seconds remaining in the first half and New York trailing 14–7, Manning directed the offense on a seven-play, 71-yard march that silenced the crowd and trampled the Cowboys' momentum. On the last play, a four-yard touchdown pass to Amani Toomer, Manning spun and pumped his fist after

the Giants tied the score. They went on to win 21–17.

At Green Bay in the NFC Championship Game, Manning whizzed passes in the frigid climate, dominating the Packers' aggressive bump-and-run coverage and outplaying a rejuvenated Brett Favre in a 23–20 overtime thriller.

But the performance that will be most celebrated by New Yorkers is his triumph over Tom Brady and New England in one of the greatest upsets in league history. In the Super Bowl he was 19 for 34 for 255 yards, two touchdowns and one interception.

In many ways Manning overcame more than just the Patriots. He withstood the unique pressures of his upbringing and beat back the suffocating clamor of a New York sports populace that had begun to wince whenever he dropped back to pass. Earlier in his career—and even during '07—each Giants loss was viewed as more evidence that the quarterback lacked what it took to be a leader of men.

The Giants had traded the rights to Philip Rivers and three draft picks to the Chargers to bring Manning to New York. In '04 rookie quarterback Ben Roethlisberger (the 11th pick) led the Pittsburgh Steelers to a 15–1 record and followed with a Super Bowl title the next year. In '06 Rivers led San Diego to a 14–2 record and was selected for his first Pro Bowl.

Manning was seen as lagging behind both, but over a four-game stretch in January and February, far from the Giants' home field in East Rutherford, N.J., Manning finally stood alone, his expectations met, his status as a New York legend secure.

"I just think he has what it takes to lead his team to championships," Peyton says. "I have always thought that. He throws the deep ball as good as anybody in the league. I find him, when I watch him on TV, getting out of a lot of tough situations. I just don't think this will be the last one for him."

Says Eli, when asked about winning in the face of doubters, "This is about this team, about the players, the coaches, everybody who has believed in us. It's not about proving anything to anybody. It is just about doing it for yourself, doing it for your teammates."

And doing it your own quiet way. □

EVERYWHERE MAN

RAISED ON THREE CONTINENTS, OSI UMENYIORA HAS BEEN A MELTING POT OF TROUBLE FOR NFL OPPONENTS

by LEE JENKINS

O SI UMENYIORA FELL ASLEEP EVERY NIGHT BENEATH A WHITE BLANKET adorned with little one-eyed men. He'd pull the cover under his chin and stare at the faces, pondering who they were and where they came from. They had patches over their right eyes and two swords crossed behind their heads. They wore silver helmets with a black stripe down the center. Umenyiora wondered why they needed the helmets. ¶ The blanket was a gift from his stepmother, Ijeoma, who'd picked it up on a trip to the U.S. and took it home to Lagos, Nigeria. Young Osi loved the blanket, even if its decorative origins eluded him. "I just thought it looked cool," he says. ¶ Only after he had turned 14 and moved to the States did he make sense of those one-eyed men. Watching television on a Sunday afternoon at his new home in Auburn, Ala., Umenyiora stopped on a channel showing athletes running into each other. Two teams were playing American football. One was wearing silver-and-black helmets, with those same little men on the sides—patches over their right eyes, swords crossed behind their heads. "I finally realized then who they were," Umenyiora says. "The Oakland Raiders." ¶ It was the beginning of an accelerated Western education. Born in London and raised in Nigeria, the 26-year-old defensive end, who had 13 of the Giants' league-leading 53 sacks

Umenyiora, a defensive end, has led the Giants in sacks for four straight seasons.

||| Photograph by JEROME DAVIS/ICON SMI

this season, is an ideal representative of New York, a mash-up of cultures. Ask him where he comes from, and he hesitates. His passport says the United Kingdom. His family is from Nigeria. His pass-rush skills are from the Deep South. After spending seven years in each place, his accent has hints of cockney, Ibo and Southern drawl. "I feel like I come from everywhere," says Umenyiora, who now splits time between Atlanta and Edgewater, N.J. "But I've taken something different from all the places I've lived. I try to represent all of them to the fullest."

He is royalty from New York to Nigeria. Umenyiora's father, John, a retired telecommunications contractor, is a king in the village of Ogbunike, which makes Osi a reluctant prince. Last off-season, when Umenyiora returned to Nigeria for the first time since he left as a teen, the villagers made him an honorary chief—not for his football achievements but because of the 30 scholarships he endows each year for local schoolchildren. "It was a huge party," says Umenyiora's older brother Ejimofor. "There was a lot of music and dancing. It was very unusual for someone so young to be a chief."

Umenyiora earned his second Pro Bowl nod this season and made almost $6 million. But his gridiron success is largely an accident. He grew up in England playing soccer. When he was seven, his family moved to Nigeria, and he played more soccer. But his father believed his children could get a better education in the U.S., so Osi traveled to Auburn to live with Ejimofor and his older sister Nkem, who was attending nearby Tuskegee University.

Osi had no urge to play football, but in Alabama a 14-year-old who weighs almost 250 pounds does not have much choice. He went out for the team when he was 15 and a junior at Auburn High. "The first day, I remember everybody was on the field for practice—except Osi," says Clay McCall, then the school's defensive line coach. "I went to the locker room and saw him standing there with his pads next to him. He didn't know how to put them on."

He learned quickly and played extensively that year. But early in his senior season Umenyiora quit. Ejimofor

and Nkem had pulled their brother off the team, believing football was the cause of his slipping grades. Osi spent two weeks pleading before they begrudgingly let him return. "The way we were brought up, sports was not a form of employment," Ejimofor says. "It was a form of recreation. I was totally against letting him play football. But in hindsight I guess it was a good decision."

Having drawn no interest from recruiters, Umenyiora was planning to enroll at Auburn. But when he saw Tracy Rocker, a scout from then Division I-AA Troy, in the hallway at his school, he introduced himself. "I

"IF YOU DON'T GET OFF THE BALL FAST— *REALLY* FAST— HE'S ALREADY AROUND YOU," SAYS VETERAN EAGLE WILLIAM THOMAS.

Soul mates Strahan (above, left) and Umenyiora form a formidable Giants tandem.

am going to play for you," Umenyiora said. Rocker, a former All-America defensive lineman at Auburn, was too startled to laugh. He watched tape of Umenyiora and came away nonplussed. Umenyiora did not get to the quarterback. He did not make tackles. But he also never stopped chasing the ballcarrier, never stopped running. "If he was willing to do that," Rocker says, "I was willing to give him a chance."

Umenyiora red-shirted as a 16-year-old freshman at Troy, then shuttled between tackle and end for the next two seasons. Coaches remember the day he found his groove: Oct. 19, 2002, the eighth game of his senior year. Troy was playing at Marshall, and Umenyiora was lined up across from Steve Sciullo, a future NFL draft pick who hadn't given up a sack in two years. The week leading up to the game, Troy defensive ends coach Mike Pelton taunted Umenyiora, "No sacks in two years."

In the second quarter Umenyiora sprinted around Sciullo and tackled quarterback Byron Leftwich. As Umenyiora ran to the sideline, he howled, "I got him! I got him!" By the end of the season Umenyiora had a school-record 16 sacks and was an NFL prospect. "That game changed everything," Pelton says. "It was the moment he took off."

Back in Nigeria, no one understood. Umenyiora's

Osi channeled LT against the Eagles in Week 4 (above), sacking McNabb six times, but off the field his intensity gives way to a playful persona (right).

mother, Chinelo Chukwueke, had never seen him play. His father had come to Troy to watch a game, but it was so cold he never got out of his car. His large family was just learning the word *sack*.

Though Umenyiora was not invited to the NFL combine in 2003, Giants G.M. Ernie Accorsi drafted him in the second round. A year later, when Accorsi was negotiating the famous draft-day trade with the Chargers for quarterback Eli Manning, San Diego asked that Umenyiora be included in the package. Accorsi refused.

"It would have been a deal-breaker," Accorsi says. "There was no way I was going to trade Umenyiora."

In Umenyiora, New York found a bookend, and soul mate, for Michael Strahan. Like Umenyiora, Strahan was raised overseas, in Germany. And like Umenyiora, Strahan played college football in relative obscurity, at Texas Southern. As a rookie Umenyiora was asked to perform a skit impersonating a veteran teammate. He chose to mimic a Strahan sack. The reviews were glowing—except from Strahan.

"I don't think he liked it," Umenyiora said. "I actually thought he was really mean at first. But the more we talked, the more we realized we are almost the same person."

With Strahan rushing from the left and Umenyiora from the right, opponents have not known whom to double-team. In Week 4 the Eagles assigned primary responsibility for Umenyiora to 6' 6" left tackle Winston Justice, who was making his second start, in place of injured veteran William Thomas. Watching on television, Thomas was concerned. "When you're going up against Osi, he lines up really wide, about three or four feet away from you," Thomas says. "He gets down low in that sprinter's stance and takes a running start. If you don't get off the ball fast—*really* fast—he's already around you."

That night Umenyiora was the second coming of Lawrence Taylor. He raced around Justice for one sack, then another, and another. Philadelphia tried chipping him with a running back. They slid their protection toward him. But he kept finding quarterback Donovan McNabb. The 6' 3", 261-pound Umenyiora got so tired from sacking McNabb that he needed an IV before halftime.

On the way to the locker room for the treatment, he saw Taylor standing on the sideline. The two had never met. Umenyiora nodded. Taylor nodded back. "It was an amazing moment," Umenyiora says. "It was like I had his spirit inside of me." He finished the night with six sacks, one short of the NFL record.

That game inspired hope in New York and fear in

the Patriots, a fear that was realized with the Giants' historic upset in Super Bowl XLII. And now Umenyiora has one more game to play. He is going to the Pro Bowl, and his parents are coming along. His mother saw him play for the first time in October, when the Giants faced the Dolphins in London. His father will be watching too—assuming, of course, it's not too cold in Hawaii.

After that Umenyiora plans to return to Lagos and to Ogbunike. He will be greeted as a prince and a chief, but he is not comfortable with those titles. He prefers to be known simply as a Brit, an African and a Southerner, the havoc wreaker who comes at you from everywhere. □

Blue Blood

MICHAEL STRAHAN IS THE MAN AMONG GIANTS

MICHAEL STRAHAN *likes to talk. "He talks so much," says fellow defensive end Justin Tuck, "that some stuff just goes in one ear and out the other." Tuck is kidding, of course, and will be the first to admit that his gregarious teammate of three years is worth listening to more often than not. "Off the field he is a guy that you can definitely talk to. It doesn't even have to be about football—just about life. He has steered us in the right direction."*

Last July it looked as if the Giants might have lost their defensive rudder when Strahan didn't report to training camp. Rumors started flying. The reasons for his absence were debated for weeks, but Strahan later explained that he just didn't have "that feeling" that drove him to stalk opposing quarterbacks week after week.

As it turned out, the feeling hadn't completely gone, and Strahan—who signed with the Giants' organization as an underestimated second-round draft pick out of Texas Southern in 1993—rejoined the team five days before the 2007 season opener and was soon voted one of five team captains. "That was amazing," admits Strahan. "I truly didn't expect it because I hadn't been there."

Rookie defensive back Aaron Ross wasn't surprised by the team's decision—and he had barely even met Strahan. "He stands up and lets us know what's in his heart," says the 25-year-old Ross, who grew up playing Strahan in NFL video games. "It's very valuable to see a veteran playing around with the younger guys."

Strahan, 36, hasn't always found it easy to smile during his career. In '99 he was criticized for not playing as if he was worth his new $8 million-a-year contract, the richest deal an NFL defensive lineman had ever received. In '04

The NFC championship victory over the Packers gave Strahan another shot to win the Super Bowl.

he sat out eight games after tearing a muscle in his chest, and sordid details of the pending divorce from his wife, Jean, made New York tabloid headlines in '05. The season after that, he missed six games with a foot injury.

But in '07 Strahan played all 20 games. He didn't come close to matching the record-breaking 22½-sack season he'd had in '01, but his strong supporting cast made double-teaming him costly. Strahan (nine sacks), Osi Umenyiora (13) and Tuck (10) combined for 60.4% of the Giants' league-leading 53 sacks.

An injury-free and noticeably more carefree Strahan was one of the reasons the Giants were loose in '07. "I am not under any pressure to please anybody except myself," says Strahan, who lightened the mood in one particularly tense huddle this season by calling the defensive backs "the ugliest group" he'd ever played with in his career.

"They were mad," Strahan said with his trademark, gap-toothed grin, "because they thought I was going to say something philosophical about the game."

He does that, too, when the situation calls for it. As the only player besides Amani Toomer who remained from the Giants' Super Bowl XXXV team, Strahan was asked by coach Tom Coughlin to help prepare the younger guys and let them know what to expect in Arizona. Strahan told his teammates to enjoy the moment, relax and remember that it's just a game of football, advice he hasn't always heeded himself.

"When you're young, you go, Oh, man, my shoe didn't tie the right way, so maybe I'm going to be a little off today," Strahan says with feigned distress. "I just go out and make sure that the way I play and what I say on the sideline always inspires everybody else." —Elizabeth McGarr

CONGRATULATIONS!

to the NY Giants • 2008 Champions
from the A&P Family of Supermarkets

JENNINGS

BROWN

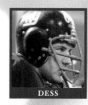
DESS

PARCELLS

HEIN

NEW YORK'S FINEST

The only thing more difficult than assembling this list of Giants would be trying to stop them on the field Compiled by PETE McENTEGART

OFFENSE

QB PHIL SIMMS 1979–93	Super Bowl XXI MVP (22 for 25) holds almost every major franchise passing record
RB TIKI BARBER 1997–2006	Versatile back is Giants rushing leader (10,449 yards) and second in receptions (586)
RB FRANK GIFFORD* 1952–60, '62–64	1956 NFL MVP named to seven Pro Bowls at three positions (HB, DB and WR)
WR DEL SHOFNER 1961–67	Deep threat (18.1 yards per catch) selected to the All-NFL team of the 1960s
WR AMANI TOOMER 1996–PRESENT	Dependable WR is team leader in catches, receiving yards and receiving TDs
TE MARK BAVARO 1985–90	Bullish blocker twice led team in receptions, including 66 in '86 for the Super Bowl champs
T ROOSEVELT BROWN* 1953–65	A 27th-round draft pick, he was named All-NFL eight straight seasons
T STEVE OWEN* 1926–31, '33	Four-time All-NFL two-way star later coached Giants to two NFL titles
G JACK STROUD 1953–64	Made three Pro Bowls at guard before moving to tackle on perennially contending teams
G DARRELL DESS 1959–64, '66–69	*Esquire* cover subject (October '65) named to two Pro Bowls while flanking Brown
C MEL HEIN* 1931–45	Only center to be named NFL MVP, in '38, he never missed a game while playing both ways

DEFENSE

DE MICHAEL STRAHAN 1993–PRESENT	NFL's single-season sack king also holds the Giants' career mark (141/2)
DE ANDY ROBUSTELLI* 1956–64	Defensive leader helped team get to six title games and was All-NFL five times as Giant
DT ARNIE WEINMEISTER* 1950–53	Made All-NFL in each of four seasons with team before he was lured to Canadian Football League
LB LAWRENCE TAYLOR* 1981–93	Revolutionized position—and helped popularize 3–4 defense—with his blazing pass rush
LB SAM HUFF* 1956–63	Helped glamorize the role of middle linebacker as football gained popularity on television
LB HARRY CARSON* 1976–88	Heart of '86 Super Bowl defense reached nine Pro Bowls, just one fewer than LT
LB CARL BANKS 1984–92	Overshadowed by LT, steady outside 'backer was key member of two Super Bowl champs
CB DICK LYNCH 1959–66	Longtime Giants radio voice twice led the NFL in interceptions ('61, '63)
CB MARK COLLINS 1986–93	Underrated cover man twice named All-NFL, started for two Super Bowl winners
S EMLEN TUNNELL* 1948–58	Team's first black player made nine Pro Bowls, had 74 interceptions as a Giant
S JIMMY PATTON 1955–66	Like Robustelli and Huff, played on all six Eastern Conference champs from '56 to '63

SPECIAL TEAMS

P DAVE JENNINGS 1974–84	Four-time Pro Bowl pick one of few bright spots on largely forgettable Giants teams
K PETE GOGOLAK 1966–74	Franchise scoring leader (646 points) blazed trail for soccer-style booters
PR/KR DAVE MEGGETT 1989–94	Giants' alltime leader in punt return yardage (2,230), second in kickoffs (2,989)
Coach BILL PARCELLS 1983–90	The Tuna helped resuscitate long-dormant Giants pride while winning two Super Bowls

*Hall of Famer

GREA
GIANTS OF

LAWRENCE TAYLOR

LB | CAREER: 1981–93

HIGHLIGHTS: *Made 10 straight Pro Bowls, from 1981 to '90, setting an NFL record*

When Taylor retired, he was No. 2 alltime on the NFL's career sack list. LT had his finest season in 1986, with a career-high 20½ sacks and 105 tackles. He was named MVP of the league that year as the Giants went on to win the Super Bowl.

||| Photograph by JOHN BIEVER

TEST
ALL TIME

TOTAL
6
7

FRANK GIFFORD

RB | CAREER: 1952-60, '62-64
HIGHLIGHT: *1956 NFL MVP*

The versatile Gifford still holds the Giants' record for touchdowns (78) and is second in yards per rush with at least 500 attempts (4.3). He totaled 9,862 combined yards for his career and scored 484 points, which ranks third in franchise history. Before finishing his career as a flanker, Gifford threw 14 TDs in his halfback heyday.

||| Photograph by MARVIN E. NEWMAN

PHIL SIMMS

QB | CAREER: 1979-93   **HIGHLIGHT:** *MVP of Super Bowl XXI*

During his 15-year career Simms had a .597 winning percentage (95-64, including 6-4 in the postseason) as a starter. He still holds 19 franchise records, and his 2,576 completions in 4,647 attempts for 33,462 yards are alltime Giants marks. Simms threw for more than 300 yards in a game 21 times during his career.

||| Photograph by JOHN IACONO

ANDY ROBUSTELLI

DE | CAREER: 1956-64
HIGHLIGHTS: *Played in eight NFL title games*

One of the finest pass rushers the NFL has ever seen, Robustelli was also one of the most durable, missing just one game in 14 seasons. In 1962 he became the first defender selected by the Maxwell Club as the league's most outstanding player.

||| Photograph by HY PESKIN

EMLEN TUNNELL
S | CAREER: 1948–58
HIGHLIGHTS: *Named NFL's alltime safety in 1969; six-time All-NFL and nine-time Pro Bowler*

During the '52 season Tunnell gained more yards (924) on interceptions and kick returns than did the NFL's rushing leader (894). He was a key player on the Giants' famed umbrella defense.

||| Photograph by BETTMANN/CORBIS

SAM HUFF
LB | CAREER: 1956–63
HIGHLIGHTS: *Played in five Pro Bowls and was named All-NFL four times*

Drafted in the third round out of West Virginia, Huff became an immediate star at middle linebacker during a glamour era for defense, anchoring a unit that helped the Giants reach the championship game six times in an eight-year period.

||| Photograph by NEIL LEIFER

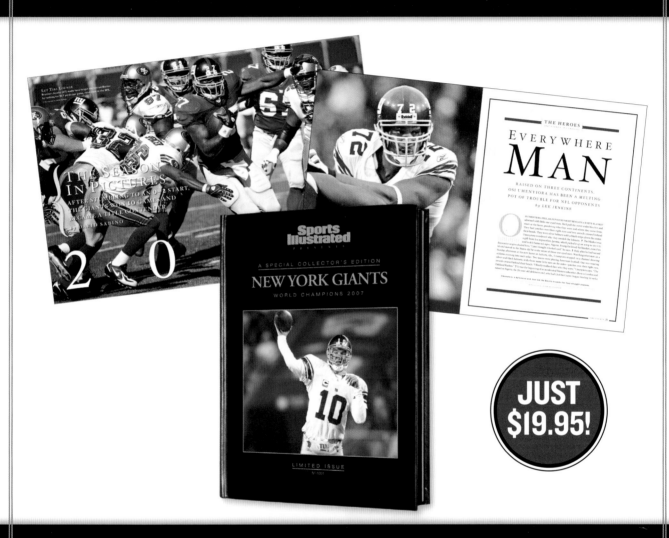

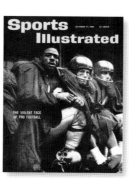

DECEMBER 3, 1956
Chuck Conerly was the first
Giant face on an SI cover.

OCTOBER 24, 1960
Roosevelt Brown blocked his
way into the Hall of Fame.

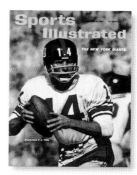

NOVEMBER 20, 1961
Legendary Y.A. Tittle led the
Giants to three Eastern titles.

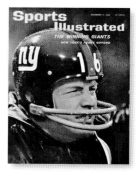

DECEMBER 17, 1962
Frank Gifford was closing out
a celebrated career.

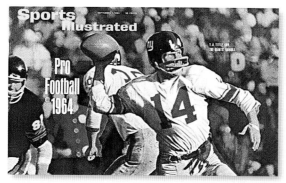

SEPTEMBER 7, 1964
YAT closed his HOF career wearing Giants red, white and blue.

JULY 17, 1967
"Scramblin' Fran" Tarkenton, prototype of the mobile QB, was
as much of a threat on the ground as he was through the air.

DECEMBER 15, 1986
Nicknamed Rambo for his toughness, Mark Bavaro was
a favorite target of Phil Simms' during the '86 title season.

JANUARY 26, 1987
Linebacker Lawrence Taylor
terrorized many an offense.

FEBRUARY 2, 1987
Simms completed 22 of 25
passes in Super Bowl XXI.

FIFTY YEARS OF FRONT-PAGE BLUES

THE COVERS OF SPORTS ILLUSTRATED TELL THE STORY OF THE GIANTS *Compiled by* FIDENCIO ENRIQUEZ

To order photo reprints of your favorite SI cover, go to SIcovers.com.

SEPTEMBER 9, 1987
The '87 season was a complete 180 for the Giants.

JANUARY 28, 1991
The Giants were considered long shots to win the trophy . . .

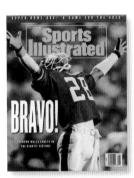

FEBRUARY 4, 1991
. . . but they edged Buffalo for a second Super Bowl triumph.

JULY 21, 1997
Frank Gifford 35 years later: still a picture of greatness.

JANUARY 22, 2001
The G Men routed Minnesota for a Super Bowl berth.

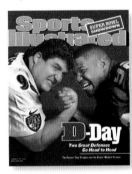

JANUARY 29, 2001
The Baltimore D denied the Giants a third Super victory.

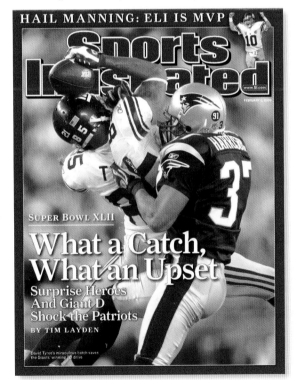

FEBRUARY 11, 2008
David Tyree's miracle catch following Eli Manning's mad scramble kept alive the drive that put New York in Big Blue heaven.

JANUARY 28, 2008
The Giants surprised three teams to make the big show . . .

FEBRUARY 4, 2008
. . . but could they ruin New England's perfect run?

FOR THE

TELLING NUMBERS AND KEY STATS FROM THE

2007 REGULAR-SEASON STATISTICS

WILSON

TOOMER

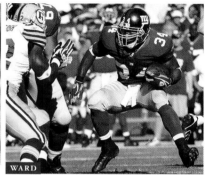

WARD

PASSING

PLAYER	ATT	COMP	PCT	YDS	TD	INT	LONG	RATING
Eli MANNING	529	297	56.1	3,336	23	20	60	73.9
Jared LORENZEN	8	4	50.0	28	0	0	9	58.3
Anthony WRIGHT	7	1	14.3	12	0	0	12	39.6

RUSHING

PLAYER	ATT	YDS	YDS/ATT	LONG	TD
Brandon JACOBS	202	1,009	5.0	43	4
Derrick WARD	125	602	4.8	44	3
Reuben DROUGHNS	85	275	3.2	45	6
Ahmad BRADSHAW	23	190	8.3	88	1
Eli MANNING	29	69	2.4	18	1
Jeremy SHOCKEY	1	6	6	6	0
Sinorice MOSS	1	4	4	4	0
Jared LORENZEN	1	2	2	2	0
Anthony WRIGHT	1	-1	-1	-1	0
Domenik HIXON	1	-8	-8	-8	0

RECEIVING

PLAYER	REC	YDS	YDS/REC	LONG	TD
Plaxico BURRESS	70	1,025	14.6	60	12
Amani TOOMER	59	760	12.9	40	3
Jeremy SHOCKEY	57	619	10.9	29	3
Derrick WARD	26	179	6.9	17	1
Brandon JACOBS	23	174	7.6	34	2
Sinorice MOSS	21	225	10.7	20	0
Kevin BOSS	9	118	13.1	23	2
Steve SMITH	8	63	7.9	12	0
Reuben DROUGHNS	7	49	7.0	11	0
Madison HEDGECOCK	6	45	7.5	9	0
Michael MATTHEWS	6	28	4.7	6	0
Anthony MIX	3	39	13.0	21	0
David TYREE	4	35	8.8	24	0
Ahmad BRADSHAW	2	12	6.0	11	0
Domenik HIXON	1	5	5.0	5	0

KICKING

PLAYER	FGM	FGA	LONG	XPM	XP ATT
Lawrence TYNES	23	27	48	40	42

DEFENSE

PLAYER	TT	SOLO	AST	SCK	INT
Antonio PIERCE	103	77	26	1	1
Gibril WILSON	92	78	14	0	4
Kawika MITCHELL	76	54	22	3½	1
Sam MADISON	67	59	8	1	4
Justin TUCK	65	48	17	10	0
James BUTLER	61	45	16	0	1
Michael STRAHAN	57	45	12	9	0
Osi UMENYIORA	52	40	12	13	0
Mathias KIWANUKA	46	34	12	4½	0
Kevin DOCKERY	46	31	15	0	0
Aaron ROSS	42	35	7	1½	3
Fred ROBBINS	42	31	11	5½	0
Reggie TORBOR	39	27	12	1	0
Barry COFIELD	34	29	5	1	0
Michael JOHNSON	25	23	2	0	0
Chase BLACKBURN	22	20	2	0	0
Craig DAHL	19	16	3	0	0
Corey WEBSTER	18	17	1	0	1
R.W. McQUARTERS	15	14	1	0	0
Gerris WILKINSON	14	10	4	0	0
Domenik HIXON	11	8	3	0	0
Ahmad BRADSHAW	9	9	0	0	0
David TYREE	9	7	2	0	0
Reuben DROUGHNS	7	5	2	0	0
Zak DeOSSIE	6	6	0	0	0
Russel DAVIS	5	2	3	0	0
David DIEHL	4	4	0	0	0
Dave TOLLEFSON	4	2	2	0	0
Rich SEUBERT	3	3	0	0	0
Jeremy SHOCKEY	3	3	0	0	0
Eli MANNING	2	2	0	0	0
Michael MATTHEWS	2	2	0	0	0
Amani TOOMER	2	2	0	0	0
Lawrence TYNES	2	2	0	0	0
Derrick WARD	2	2	0	0	0
Madison HEDGECOCK	2	1	1	0	0
Manuel WRIGHT	2	1	1	0	0
Plaxico BURRESS	1	1	0	0	0

RECORD

GIANTS' SUPER SEASON *Compiled by* FIDENCIO ENRIQUEZ

PLAYOFF SCOREBOARD

NFC WILD CARD
Giants vs. Buccaneers at Tampa

TEAM	IST	2ND	3RD	4TH	TOTAL
NYG	0	14	3	7	24
TB	7	0	0	7	14

RUSHING NYG: Bradshaw 17–66, Jacobs 13–34 (1 TD). TB: Graham 18–63 (1 TD), Pittman 1–5, Askew 1–3, Garcia 1–2, Galloway 1–minus 4.

PASSING NYG: Manning 20–27 for 185, 2 TDs. TB: Garcia 23–39 for 207, 1 TD, 2 INTs.

RECEIVING NYG: Toomer 7–74 (1 TD), Burress 4–38, Smith 3–29, Jacobs 2–16 (1 TD), Boss 2–14, Bradshaw 1–9, Hedgecock 1–5. TB: Pittman 5–62, Clayton 3–39, Graham 4–27, Hilliard 4–27, Smith 3–26 (1 TD), Askew 2–12, Galloway 1–9, Stevens 1–5.

NFC DIVISIONAL PLAYOFF
Giants vs. Cowboys at Irving, Texas

TEAM	IST	2ND	3RD	4TH	TOTAL
NYG	7	7	0	7	21
DAL	0	14	3	0	17

RUSHING NYG: Jacobs 14–54 (1 TD), Bradshaw 6–34, Manning 3–2. DAL: Barber 27–129 (1 TD), Romo 3–17, J. Jones 3–8.

PASSING NYG: Manning 12–18 for 163, 2 TDs. DAL: Romo 18–36 for 201, 1 TD, 1 INT.

RECEIVING NYG: Toomer 4–80 (2 TDs), Smith 4–48, Boss 1–19, Bradshaw 1–6, Burress 1–5, Jacobs 1–5. DAL: Witten 7–81, Owens 4–49 (1 TD), Glenn 2–30, Crayton 3–27, Barber 1–9, Fasano 1–5.

NFC CHAMPIONSHIP
Giants vs. Packers at Green Bay

TEAM	IST	2ND	3RD	4TH	OT	TOTAL
NYG	3	3	14	0	3	23
GB	0	10	7	3	0	20

RUSHING NYG: Jacobs 21–67 (1 TD), Bradshaw 16–63 (1 TD), Manning 2–4. GB: Grant 13–29, Favre 1–minus 1.

PASSING NYG: Manning 21–40 for 251. GB: Favre 19–35 for 236, 2 TDs, 2 INTs.

RECEIVING NYG: Burress 11–151, Toomer 4–42, Smith 2–25, Boss 1–12, Bradshaw 1–9, Jacobs 1–8, Tyree 1–4. GB: Driver 5–141 (1 TD), Lee 3–35 (1 TD), Robinson 4–16, Jennings 1–14, Hall 1–12, Franks 1–11, Morency 2–9, Jackson 1–1, Grant 1–minus 3.

SUPER BOWL XLII
Giants vs. Patriots at Glendale, Ariz.

TEAM	IST	2ND	3RD	4TH	TOTAL
NYG	3	0	0	14	17
NE	0	7	0	7	14

RUSHING NYG: Bradshaw 9–45, Jacobs 14–42, Manning 3–4. NE: Maroney 14–36, Faulk 1–7, Evans 1–2.

PASSING NYG: Manning 19–34 for 255, 2 TDs, 1 INT. NE: T. Brady 29–48 for 266, 1 TD.

RECEIVING NYG: Toomer 6–84, Smith 5–50, Boss 1–45, Tyree 3–43 (1 TD), Burress 2–27 (1 TD), Bradshaw 1–3, Hedgecock 1–3. NE: Welker 11–103, Moss 5–62 (1 TD), Faulk 7–52, Stallworth 3–34, Maroney 2–12, K. Brady 1–3.

GIANTS BY THE NUMBERS

11 NUMBER of consecutive games won on the road by the Giants, a NFL record for a single season. The streak included victories in 10 states and a stop in another country (the United Kingdom).

81,176 ATTENDANCE at London's Wembley Stadium for the Giants' 13–10 win over the Dolphins on Oct. 28. It was the first regular-season NFL game played outside North America.

53 SACKS by the Giants' defense, which led the league. This total includes 12 sacks against Philadelphia on Sept. 30, which tied an NFL record.

151 RUSHING YARDS by rookie running back Ahmad Bradshaw in the 38–21 win over Buffalo on Dec. 23, the highest total by a Giants rookie since Eddie Price ran for 156 yards against the New York Yankees on Dec. 3, 1950. Also Brandon Jacobs had 145 yards in the game, making this the first time in franchise history that the Giants had two players rush for more than 100 yards in the same game.

88 YARD RUN by Bradshaw against Buffalo, the longest in the NFL in 2007.

BOSS

620 CAREER receptions by Amani Toomer, the most in Giants history. Toomer passed Tiki Barber (586) in Week 6 against the Falcons. The receiver also holds franchise records for receiving yards (8,917), 100-yard games (22) and touchdowns (50).

1 TANDEM of brothers who have appeared at quarterback in the Super Bowl. Eli Manning's older brother Peyton was the winning QB in Super Bowl XLI last season.

8 DRAFT PICKS from 2007 who made the Giants' roster, including Kevin Boss (*above*).

65,793 CAREER punting yards by 20-year veteran Jeff Feagles, the NFL record.

5 PLAYERS in NFL history who have rushed for 1,000 yards in 11 games or fewer. Brandon Jacobs had 1,009 yards in 11 games in '07.

BROTHERS IN BLUE

by HARRY CARSON

as told to Elizabeth McGarr

WHEN YOU BECOME A GIANT, YOU FEEL LIKE YOU'RE PART OF A FAMILY. OUR OWNER, WELLINGTON MARA, TOOK AN INTEREST IN YOU AS A PLAYER AND AS A PERSON, AND WHETHER WE HAD WON OR LOST, HE WOULD COME TO THE LOCKER ROOM AND SHAKE your hand. You didn't want to disappoint the family.

And that includes the fans. If you play your heart out and lose to a superior opponent, Giants fans give you applause and say job well done, but if you go out and stink up the place, they're not very forgiving. I was there during those very lean years, the '70s and early '80s, when fans expressed their frustration by burning tickets. Then there was that plane flying overhead with the trailing banner that read 15 YEARS OF LOUSY FOOTBALL—WE'VE HAD ENOUGH. Having gone through that made winning the Super Bowl in '86 so much sweeter.

That season everything clicked in the second game, against San Diego. We had lost our first game to the Dallas Cowboys, 31–28, and San Diego had beaten Miami 50–28. Nobody really thought we could compete with the Chargers, but we played them hard, and we won the game 20–7. At that point we knew we were on our way.

I think the turning point for the '07 Giants was the Philadelphia game the last weekend of September. It was like someone turned on a light switch, and they finally understood what they needed to do to really play solid football.

We had eight guys going to the Pro Bowl on that '86 team. This year you probably don't know anyone on the offensive line or in the secondary. On the defensive line you might only know Michael Strahan and Osi Umenyiora. They're just guys who don't threaten anybody on paper, but when they get on the field, they're very powerful because they are a team. I'll take team any day over big-name guys.

Carson is impressed by how well these Giants work as a team.

||| Photograph by DAVID BERGMAN

I was asked to be an honorary captain during the Packers game, so I flew with the team to Green Bay. When we got to the hotel, I had dinner with safety Gibril Wilson, wide receiver David Tyree and safety James Butler, and I told them that during the season, every yard counts, but when you get into the postseason, it's reduced to fractions of inches.

During the game I was down on the sideline, and Brett Favre threw a pass to Donald Driver. Driver ran after the catch and scored a touchdown after Wilson just missed him. When Wilson came over to the sideline, he looked over, and he saw me. I put two fingers up—my thumb and my index finger—and I showed him a fraction of an inch. He nodded to me that he understood.

When the players took the field this season, they were playing not just for themselves but also for every Giants player who has worn the uniform. Being on the sideline in Green Bay was a special experience that took me back to when I played, because I felt that I had a stake in what was happening with the team. I'm still part of the family.   □

From 1976 through '88 Carson made the Pro Bowl nine times. He was inducted into the Pro Football Hall of Fame in '06. Now 54, Carson lives in Franklin Lakes, N.J., with his wife, Maribel, whom he married in February '07. He is the CEO and president of Harry Carson Inc., a sports consulting company he founded in '86, and the executive director of the Fritz Pollard Alliance, an organization dedicated to creating diversity and promoting equal opportunity for nonplayers who work in the NFL.

SCORE A BIG ONE FOR THE ROAD WARRIORS.

Congratulations, Big Blue, from your friends and official airline of the NY Giants.

continental.com

Continental Airlines

Work Hard.
Fly Right.